EXPERIMENTS WITH

MATERIALS

Written by
Mignonne Gunasekara

My First EXPERIMENTS

KidHaven PUBLISHING

Published in 2022 by
KidHaven Publishing, an Imprint of Greenhaven Publishing, LLC
29 East 21st Street
New York, NY 10010

Edited by: John Wood
Designed by: Brandon Mattless

Cataloging-in-Publication Data

Names: Gunasekara, Mignonne.
Title: Experiments with materials / Mignonne Gunasekara.
Description: New York : KidHaven Publishing, 2022. | Series: My first experiments | Includes glossary and index.
Identifiers: ISBN 9781534538764 (pbk.) | ISBN 9781534538788 (library bound) | ISBN 9781534538771 (6 pack) | ISBN 9781534538795 (ebook)
Subjects: LCSH: Materials--Experiments--Juvenile literature. | Materials--Properties--Juvenile literature. | Materials--Juvenile literature.
Classification: LCC TA403.2 G858 2022 | DDC 620.11--dc23

Printed in the United States of America

CPSIA compliance information: Batch #CSKH22: For further information contact Greenhaven Publishing LLC, New York, New York at 1-844-317-7404.

Please visit our website, www.greenhavenpublishing.com. For a free color catalog of all our high-quality books, call toll free 1-844-317-7404 or fax 1-844-317-7405.

PHOTO CREDITS

Images are courtesy of Shutterstock.com. With thanks to Getty Images, Thinkstock Photo, and iStockphoto.

Cover – sirikorn thamniyom, Kingcraft. Recurring Images (cover and internals) – Buntoon (background pattern), The_Pixel (grid), balabolk (headers and vectors), wildfloweret (boxes), Steve Paint (arrows), yana shypova (speech bubbles), Tsaranna (vector frames and boxes). p1 – sirikorn thamniyom, p4–5 – yadom, Andrey Eremin, Butterfly Hunter, p6–7 – In Green, JIANG HONGYAN, kai keisuke, Lapina Maria, Sakdinon Kadchiangsaen, Tarasyuk Igor, Valentin Valkov, p8–9 – Boris Medvedev, Littlekidmoment, KK Tan, Anton Starikov, Jag_cz, p10–11 – Ligux_f, p12–13 – Marta navarroP, p14–15 – M.Scherbyna, Yuganov Konstantin, Zurijeta, p16–17 – raevas, Salienko Evengii, Nazarova Mariia, p18–19 – GUNDAM_Ai, StockSmartStart, p20–21 – Steve Cukrov, p22–23 – Dean Drobot, Andrey Eremin, Butterfly Hunter.

CONTENTS

Words that look like <u>this</u> can be found in the glossary on page 24.

Hello, SCIENTISTS!

Science is about learning why and how everything works. A scientist's job is to find the answers to those questions.

We are going to be learning about materials today. Science will help us with that, and we'll carry out some fun experiments along the way.

If you complete the experiments, you will earn your Materials Badge!

Marvelous MATERIALS

Here are some materials you may have heard of.

All the objects around you are made of materials. Each material is different, which is why they are chosen to do certain jobs.

Plastic

Rock

Metal

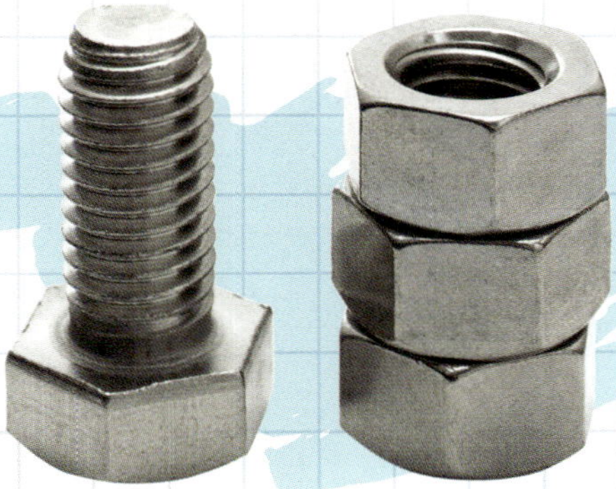

Glass

Wood

Fabric

Some materials are hard and some are soft. Some materials are rough and some are smooth. Materials can be human-made, such as plastic, or natural, such as rock.

Glass is hard and usually smooth.

Fabric is soft.

Metals can be hard or soft.

Pure gold is a very soft metal. You can even bend it with your bare hands!

Experiment:

LAVA LAMP

Oil and water are two materials that don't mix together.

Let's use them to make a lava lamp!

Materials:

- A clear plastic bottle or glass jar
- Water
- Vegetable oil or baby oil
- Food coloring
- Denture-cleaning tablets or table salt
- Glitter
- A flashlight

You may need to ask an adult for help - things could get messy!

1) Fill up the bottle or jar with water until it is one-quarter full.

2) Fill the rest of the bottle or jar with the oil. Leave a bit of space at the top and let the layers settle.

3) Add a couple of drops of food coloring.

4) Add glitter at this stage, if you'd like.

5) Break two denture-cleaning tablets into small pieces and drop them in. If you don't have any of these tablets, you can pour some table salt in.

6) Your lava lamp is ready!

7) You can shine a flashlight through the bottom of the bottle or jar to make it light up.

When you're done, you can put a lid on your bottle or jar to store it until you want to use it again. Just add more tablets or salt when you want more lava!

Extra questions:

What happens if you put the lid on your container the minute you put your tablet or salt in?

What happens if you drop a whole tablet in, instead of broken pieces of tablets?

Get to WORK

Materials such as plastic, metal, and wood are usually strong. This makes them good for building.

Glass is used to make windows because you can see through it.

Raincoats, umbrellas, and rain boots are made from waterproof materials, so you don't get wet.

Making MATERIALS

Natural materials are found in nature. Metals and rocks are found in the ground, and we can get them out by mining. Wood comes from trees.

Mining for limestone, a type of rock

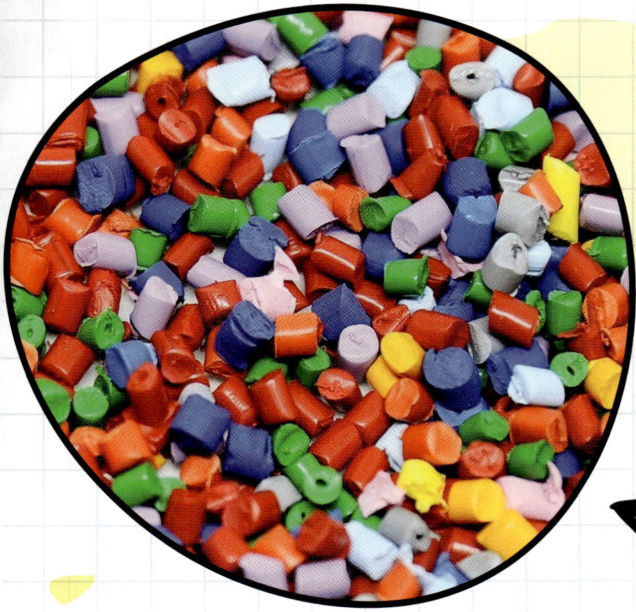

Human-made materials, such as plastic, are not found in nature. They are often made in factories.

Plastic pellets

My grandma knitted this scarf out of sheep's wool!

Sometimes, a material is natural but needs a little human help to become useful – such as sheep's wool.

Ready, Set, RECYCLE

Recycling is really important. We can use materials again instead of making more.

Ask an adult to help you find out which materials can be recycled at your local recycling center.

Glass, paper, some plastics, and some metals can be recycled.

Experiment: CRACKING Up!

This is a group experiment. You will need eggs, clear tape, and lots of different materials. This could get messy, so ask an adult first.

1 – Have everyone take a raw egg.

2 – Wrap your egg in a material to protect it.

3 – Use tape to hold the wrapping in place.

You could try these materials: cardboard, paper, bubble wrap, fabric, sponge, empty toilet paper rolls.

4 – Everybody drops their protected eggs from the same height.

5 – Make a note of the materials you used and what happened to the eggs in a table like this:

Name	Egg Cracked?	Material	Height of Drop
Liam	No	Bubble wrap	3 feet

How many eggs cracked? Which materials protected the eggs best?

The Badge CEREMONY

You've completed the experiments – well done! You've earned your Materials Badge!

MATERIALS

GLOSSARY

experiments tests done to explore and try new things

factories buildings where things are made, usually by machines

human-made created by humans and not natural

mining digging in the ground for useful things such as metal

natural found in nature and not made by people

objects things that you can see and touch

raw uncooked

recycling using again to make something new

waterproof does not let water through

INDEX